LOVE FROM THE OUTER BANDS

LOVE
from the
OUTER BANDS

Mary Block

THE WORD WORKS
CELEBRATING 50 YEARS

Love from the Outer Band © 2025 Mary Block

Reproduction of any part of this book in any form
or by any means, electronic or mechanical,
except when quoted in part for the
purpose of review, must be
with permission in writing
from the publisher.
Address inquiries
directly to:

THE WORD WORKS
P.O. Box 42164
Washington, D.C. 20015
editor@wordworksbooks.org

No part of this book may be used
or reproduced in any manner
for the purpose of training
artificial intelligence
technologies
or systems.
Ever.

Author photograph: Christine Frigo
Cover design: Susan Pearce
Cover art: Ali Mac

ISBN: 978-1-944585-87-7

Acknowledgments

Grateful acknowledgment is given to the following publications, where these poems—some in earlier versions—first appeared:

Aquifer: The Florida Review Online: "Cocoplum"
Bellevue Literary Review: "It Comes in Waves"
Mudfish: "To A Version of Myself and to Her Mother"
Nimrod International Journal: "After It Rained"
Raleigh Review: "Mother of Pearl"
Rattle: "Crown for a Young Marriage"
RHINO: "Allegory with Human Host"
Sonora Review: "Movements of the Scapula"
Swamp Ape Review: "The Mind Is Its Own Place"
SWWIM Every Day: "I Want Some Land" and "Paloma"
Tampa Review: "Looking Down"
Weave: "Lakeland"

Best New Poets 2020: "After Rebmann and the Safari Collection Brochure"

Fevers, Feuds and Diamonds: Ebola and the Ravages of History by Paul Farmer (Farrar, Straus and Giroux, 2020): selection from "Crown for a Young Marriage"

Contents

Allegory With Human Host / 1

ONE

To a Version of Myself and to Her Mother / 5
Paloma / 7
The Boy in the Backyard / 8
The Mind Is Its Own Place / 9
Diluvian Blessing / 10
It Comes in Waves / 11
Movements of the Scapula / 12

TWO

Crown for a Young Marriage / 15

THREE

It's Your Misfortune and None of My Own / 25
Never Adopt, Says the Cabdriver / 26
Panic Attack on an Airplane, With My Daughter / 27
Mother of Pearl / 29
Turn Toward the Sun / 30
A Fish With an X for an Eye / 31
Ethel, Miami, 1967 / 33
Pietà / 35
After It Rained / 37

FOUR

Like Teenagers / 41
Crown Club Nights / 42
Rock Show in the Basement of St. Ignatius / 43
A Little Phrase, Designed to Go Unnoticed / 44
Last Drink With Dr. Manning / 45
Xanthelasmata / 46
Flatland Tours / 47
Florida Field Guide / 48
Cocoplum / 49
Hale-Bopp / 50

FIVE
    Looking Down / 55
    I Want Some Land / 56
    South of Marler / 57
    After Rebmann and the Safari Collection Brochure / 58
    Shake It / 59
    My Body Writes Me a Sonnet / 61
    Shelter As a Family / 62
    Big Sugar / 64
    Retired Hurricane Names / 65

NOTES / 69
About the Author / 71
Special Thanks / 72
About The Word Works / 74
Other Word Works Books / 75

*This book is dedicated to my mother, Jennie Weiss Block.
In every way imaginable, I owe her my life.*

Allegory With Human Host

Trust me like the little dog has to,
having been so denatured.
Having so little to do
with a wolf. Follow me
to a sinking city
where the weather hums,
where the leaves grow monster-wide.

I put my faith in larvicide
and lizards, in the tongues of frogs.
I built a house from salt
and fossil shells.

Outside the bullfrog sings
for his bride, for the mouse
and the limp-tailed rat.
The tail of a cat or some animal flicks
at the slats of our bedroom window.

I told our boy, in so many words,
the fate of foxes.
I told him the tree frog is a friend—
that even poison has its place.
But still he woke with a red ring rising
from his side.

A ring of roses is either an amulet
or an ornament. Either way
I hung a wreath outside our door.

I said trust me like the little dog has to.
Trust me, son, to be the mother
that all soft animals require
and the little dog laughed.

ONE

To a Version of Myself and to Her Mother

I was born days late, under the dog star
to a young girl who'd been lugging
an unwanted child through the last days
of Florida's August.
I had a disposable name,
just a sound for nurses to make
for three days at a baby
between two mothers—
the nurse on the night shift
holding my body
so the girl could sleep and bleed.

I know she gave birth at the Catholic hospital
under a miniature, mangled Christ.
Her story, like mine, is full of holes
and mine is full of half-remembered faces,
random phantom flares of shame.
And I know what night sounds like in that hospital.
I know she left like I did, but empty—
wheeled through Maternity like a parade.

We don't tell our daughters how much
will be expected of them by the lonely.
There are the wards of the ward—
the babies between two lives,
their ex-mothers, the hang-dog boys.
The quieter rooms, still smelling
like all the others, of animal birth.
They still have to be seen.
To be cleaned.

There is, or there was, a girl
who held my body or didn't
before handing me to the nurse
and the state of Florida,

signing whatever my name was
and hers and sealing the record.
I owe her my gift for clean breaks,
for revision. I owe her
this life and its inversion,
the one we've stored with the county clerk,
the little lacuna, the absent cradle
on every page.

Paloma

A little bitter, like eating a grapefruit
with my grandfather,
with his tiny, toothy knife
designed for the job.
A father of daughters, he'd learned
how to eat without wincing.
He knew how to leave for work.
How to leave the girls at home.

The boys catch barracuda
in a boat roaring back at the ocean
cracking against its rigid hull.
This city was built to defy the weather.
It was pulled from the sea
by boat builders in exile—
people raised with the knowledge
that pigeon and dove are two shades
of the same bird.

Between my dreams I tried to remember
the name for a lookout.
Nest came back to me first, then crow.
I blessed my boy with the flesh
of a sour fruit, with salt,
with the sign of the cross.
The school has hired a guard with a gun
but still. I fed my boy my body
for so long.

The Boy in the Backyard

> "The Florida Speleological Society has likened the state's geology to 'Swiss cheese coated with soil.'"—David Owen, *The New Yorker*

Finchy, maybe, and birdboned
or squat and low, filling more

of the hole, as I would've, surely,
I don't know, but swallowed, certainly,

while you were playing "pull the plump
roots from under asparagus ferns" or

"crush the squiggly mounds piped up
by earthworms" or some other kind

of playalone game when the sink-
pocked earth below you gave, a fret

I bet your mother never entertained:
that what she'd given you was porous,

weak and indiscriminate, swigging
tractors houses and boys

when the strawberry crop dried out
and the farmers piped up the aquifer

floating the land and her house on its top
like the crust on a crème brûlée,

that a neighbor would hear you yelp and catch
your fingertips as they passed grass-level,

that she'd set up her life on a sinkhole,
that even the ground can fail.

The Mind Is Its Own Place

We steal mangoes from the church
and say that we save them from rot,
from rats in the little chapel built
for poorly attended funerals.
Starting in June we can hear
the hurricanes being born
off the coast of Africa.
I say we, of course, meaning you,
meaning make this your problem, too.

I grew up here
on the edge of annihilation,
east of a disaffected sun,
the cover of *Time* in '81 divulging the details
of our municipal fall from grace—
the morgues at capacity,
skyscrapers built on drugs,
built to bend, like the trees, in the wind.

I know how to start over.
But these months are rough,
even on the natives,
and this one coming's a classic Cape Verde,
gathering fury above the Antilles
and pivoting north, toward home—
a city built over mounds of ancient bones.

How well have I lashed us
to this ill-fated slip of the continent?
We keep our documents wrapped in plastic.
The names of our children are marked
with the seal of the state of the stateless,
the meagerly mourned. They were born
like we all are—slicked in our mothers,
moving by touch through the dark
and whatever is in the water.

Diluvian Blessing

May the road rise up to meet you
when the tide defeats the town.
May you find a way
to get your kids to Georgia.
May the wind die down.
May the sun show you mercy,
the former inhabitant
of an elaborate circuit
of thermally optimized dwellings
and automobiles.
May the rain fall soft
on your broken city,
pitch black, dazzling
in its downed power lines,
volatile snakeheads
sparking and snapping,
hissing at legions
of disinterred dinosaurs,
liquefied, blooming
from the exhaust pipe
of a surrendering god
on his way to the state line,
hands at ten and two.

It Comes in Waves

You hear yourself contracting.
Like a horror movie drone—
like sheet metal flexing
near a microphone,
the body wrings itself.

You watch the birds
from a window in triage
for hours, spine
like a convex cat
while you wait.
The hospital halls turn gray.

You move in the ancient way,
your body eager to burst—
a limbic undulation, dark to dark,
the rhythm of the veins.

You fill a room with the remains
of the pregnancy—
clots, the placenta
still pulsing in the tray,
still so devoted.

You hold your son,
lobbed into your stunned lap
like a fish, like a flash
before he's shuttled
to the warmer.

You don't want him back.
Or you want him back
without knowing him,
or what sort of beast
you just became, what kind
of shivering animal.

Movements of the Scapula

The light turned corally.
We must have been dreaming
of falcons. Of talons. Of tiny
undulations,
a murmuration
above the intersection
of Red and Bird.
The light turned yellow.
You lifted your leather hand.
You can go. You can go.
You can fly a short distance.
You can buy the fish in the tank
and let it be your dog.
We found the bones under the house
but not the skull.
We must have been dreaming of John the Baptist.
I drank the steam
from an open manhole
while the baby slept in my womb.
Remember
the world is full of tunnels.
We are all trying to leave the house.
Remember, my son,
that we are all part water,
part sleep.

TWO

Crown for a Young Marriage

for Sean

1.

I use the built-in fan now when I cook
things on the stove. I know that mold can sprout
between the tiles at night, so now I look
for it, and try my best to scrub it out.
I've found that dish soap cleans a diamond ring
ok, that protein stains like blood and beef
come out with MSG, that everything
we've tried to flush away is underneath
the house, just waiting for a heavy rain.
I've written several hundred awful lines
for you, and wondered what you stand to gain
by staying here, and wondered if I'd mind
in looking back on how I spent my life
if I was nothing else, but was a wife.

2.

If I was nothing else, but was a wife;
If I did nothing else, but could make meals
with scraps and pantry staples and a knife
I got when I was twenty-nine; if real
commitment (an abstract and noble word
before it tangles up with sacrifice)
turns out to mean a smaller life, less heard,
less heralded, less published, and less prized;
if after spending summer days indoors
for several years, and writing frightening verse
I'm eighty-odd and pale and little more
than what I am today, will I be worse
off than my single, roving poet friends?
I doubt it, but you'll have to ask me then.

3.

I doubt it, but you'll have to ask me then.
I doubt that I'll be doddering and hunched
and wishing I could do it all again
because I felt I'd missed out on a bunch
of fellowships. And Christ, I love you. Christ
do I remember loneliness, and what
I did for scraps of evenings, what sufficed
for kindness. Offer me a life, a glut
of love, of undeserved reserves of grace
and nice interpretations of my faults.
I'll still find ways to be unhappy. Face
the facts, though—I'm at home filling the salt
shakers, cleaning the microwave, unknown.
But staunchly, resolutely unalone.

4.

A staunchly, resolutely unalone
existence is a windfall, I'm aware.
My mother, widowed young, was on her own.
She sliced a single life out of a shared
one almost overnight. She'd been one thing
at dinner but by dawn was something new,
something that no one envied. Friends would bring
us things to heat up, casseroles and stews,
and whisper thanks to Jesus for their luck
as they drove home. Our quiet, giant house
was stuffed with silence. We watched TV, stuck
our fingers in the cakes. Without a spouse,
with grieving children eating on the floor,
my mother put a brick beside her door.

5.

My mother put a brick beside her door
to keep it open. If allowed to stay
inside her room, she thought, she might unmoor.
The hours gaped, a ceaseless chug of days
that pulled us forward, toward no one knew
exactly what. I watch you rinsing fish
fillets for dinner, polishing your shoes
and wonder if I'll get to keep this. Wish
for independence, you might get it—trains
come rattling 'round their rails, a biker clicks
across a busy street. I can't explain
the terror of a grieving child, the brick
beside her mother's door, except to say
I've seen how things can change inside a day.

6.

I've seen how things can change inside a day—
a wife becomes a widow with a word;
a bride becomes a wife. A shiftless splay
of drunken string-lit evenings turns from blurred
attempts at living into life, a half-
drunk glass of wine forgotten by the bed.
We laugh at things that used to make us laugh,
we let the laundry bloom, collect the dead
bugs from the window. While we watch TV
you put your fingertip inside the scar,
a shiny crescent divot in my knee.
I stand behind you standing at the bar
to smell your collar while you order beers,
to taste the salt of sixty coming years.

7.

I taste the salt of sixty coming years,
our sprawling love asserted in a slough
of gritty flecks—that sour hope that we're
among the ones who get to get old, tough
out poorer, sicker, worse times and ascend
into a halfness, gnarled together at
the joints. We swagger home before our friends
and watch the air get thick with breath and fat,
a midnight omelette on the stove. You shove
your hair across your shiny brow and I
am rupturing with love. And since I love
in circles like a broken bird I try
to keep this, look for things I've overlooked.
I use the built-in fan now when I cook.

THREE

It's Your Misfortune and None of My Own

He said get along little dogie, get along
without judging the cow for living

her own hard life, for rejecting her calf
(a dogie not being a dog, as I'd thought,

but a castoff, a calf whose mother walks
with the herd but not with her), some quiet

animal logic leads her away from this one,
not this one, it tells her to leave her calf

to the hands, to the man singing ti-yi-yo
and rounding up strays on the north trail,

bobbing their tails and feeding them weeds
and cholla, not getting invested, insisting again

and again that he's got his own troubles,
that Mother must have had her reasons

and the only thing left to do
is keep walking, keep getting along.

Never Adopt, Says the Cabdriver.

That's not your blood.
That's not your child.
Adopted will kill you in your sleep
with a mop handle
pressed against your neck.
Adopted will tie you up
with the strings of your own guitar.

And like his car
I'm suddenly dangerous.
Strangely intimate.
Something jumped into
without enough thought.

I'm not, to this man,
just short of a secret.
A child attempting to pass
for a real child.
A second-best.
A cuckoo in the nest.
A joke between
sitcom siblings, shorthand
for Something is wrong here.
For You don't really belong here.

Panic Attack on an Airplane, With My Daughter

I start to pray but then I remember
there is no God. Philadelphia stutters
below us all in our bullet,
seatbelted, flying
inside of a cumulus hell,
hot and endless around me,
autonomic and nervous,
losing sensation, fingers taloned
around the armrest,
riding the current up and tensing
for the fall,
for the scream and the shudder
of welding, of metal kicked
through the air like a can,
like a bean, my baby,
the body I grew from a seed
strapped into this contraption,
rising and falling with me,
the mother, the maker
of this and all decisions,
wild-eyed and clawing around
for the barf bag, breathing,
the bag like a heart
pumping carbon dioxide
into my brain, getting lighter
and rising up through the holes
in my scalp and my skin,
floating over my daughter,
the vagus outline of her
in the middle seat,
next to a stranger,
tied to this thing
with its wings and fabric,
coffee and sweat suspended
in air with me, my body

below in the chair, sitting
rigid and pointless
next to my daughter,
praying to pass out,
brainless,
a primitive animal begging
to leave her young.

Mother of Pearl

A minnow circling tiny in the black,
the baby grows alone. How can I tell
you what it's like to share a body, crack
my flesh apart and feel my organs swell
with someone I don't know? How strange, to grow
a stranger. Well, I know his fishbone spine,
I've heard his stampede heart. I know that, though
I've never held him, I have hurt him. Brine
and blackness, shipwreck body, guide him home.
I pick the dog's hair off his empty bed.
We wait 'til, still more fish than child, the foam
and slime of waterlife still on his head,
we baptize him with aerosols and mites.
We make, of breathing air, a kind of rite.

Turn Toward the Sun

Tomatoes are picked green
and ripen on the truck.
Likewise a dog is ready to leave his mother
the day he stops needing her milk.
The baby cries. The dog has a defect.
His throat collapsed. He needs a stent.
I want to rid myself of my entanglements.

I picked tomatoes after school
for the food pantry.
The red ones were useless,
rotten in their eagerness.
Ambition can make you
and make you repulsive.
Puppies are sold before they are born.

Our dog is barely breathing.
I have to keep him calm.
I have to keep the baby away.
I have to have an hour alone.
The baby screams for his mother.
The puppy wheezes and trembles
in his bed.

My life is small.
I am stalled by sweetness.
I sour my own honeyed hours
with a needling, vaulting ambition,
a need to be more than what I've made.
And yes, who cares?
Who doesn't end up in the ground?
And yes, I will have meant something
to the dog.

A Fish With an X for an Eye

Too far into the recipe
to stop I saw the jellied spines
emerging
withered hunks
of silver fish skin
weeping off
I bought sardines instead
of anchovy fillets
I thought they're more
or less the same
some ochre organ now
revealed by stirring
cooked
and needing care
at this very moment
I'm suddenly totally
out of control
of my dinner
and totally aware
that there is nothing
I can do
about the hookworms in the heels
of American babies
tonight
refrigerated trucks
stacked high with mothers
here
where we're all guaranteed
the right to die
alone
I have a job
it is to make
an American dinner
for me and my children
all of us living

with something awful
something dead in the house
an animal must have died
we must have a hole
somewhere
we're all beside ourselves
and gathered around
this horrible meal
I've made
for my cartoon family
a foamy mound
a fish with an X for an eye
we're all living inside
the smell
the profound lack
of care and due diligence
right here at home

Ethel, Miami, 1967

You came down from New Orleans
with a suitcase full of kimonos.

You didn't plan much on leaving the house.
Your face had buckled, leaving you humble,

heavy and kind, but it still had beauty,
like a sinking restaurant.

You watched your body crepe in the O
of a bathroom mirror.

You felt your legs in your hipbones,
the curve of your foot on a hot glass bottle,

the sun through a sundress, the taste
of a crawfish head. You sucked

on the meat of your cheek, pinched
your skin below the jawbone.

The house did not smell like food
or spices working their way

through a woman's body.
It didn't sound like the moving patterns

of tropical bugs and their children,
eating inside the walls.

You moved the dented tin of talc
to the other side, behind the faucet.

You looked at your face, reversed,
through a constellation of toothpaste.

You came, in this wilted incarnation,
to live in a city that people

were still making up. And you still had
the whole day to fill.

Pietà

Mother Mary,
tin-eyed,
glinting at us
in your grace
from across the causeway,
make this matter.
Make it more
than degradation,
diminishing carbon,
the sum of all
his failings.

Let the room fill
with orange night
and the smell
of his mouth
like bursting plums.
Help this man remember
how to be washed,
how to be fed.
How to be shifted
in his bed.

Mother Mary,
marble hands stretched
over the hospital,
help me
to understand
the difference
between mercy
and my reluctance
to make decisions.
Hold my body
like your boy's
and let me taste

your salty cheek.
Say let it happen,
let it happen,
let it be.

After It Rained

You saw Iceland in an oil slick.
I saw lifeguards slipping, feet-first, into the sea.
You remembered the Band-Aid in the geothermal bath,
the smell of sulphur.
I remembered the floods of my youth,
the roads turning into rivers.

You say,
the cuisine of Iceland is notable for its existence.
The people there scrape a life off a mossy rock.
They bury a shark in the sand.

I say,
I am grateful to ancient fish
for the ground beneath me.
To the people who built my city
and their mosquito dead.

They built a town that could withstand the tide.
They laced their buildings into the coral bed.
They built a town that could forgive a girl
for leaving.

FOUR

Like Teenagers

in a Trans Am
at the bottom
of a lake
we waited
side by side
for years
we sprouted tendrils
from our eyes
we let our skin
dissolve
we swayed
in moonlight
slipping
through the murk
and twigs
above
us in our bodies
in the dark
like kids in love

Crown Club Nights

Spangled air suspended sweat
so thick the floor is slick
by ten o'clock you press your lips
around the rim and suck
a pink drink
let the bass in feel it
thump and thump and thump
the chest the space
your head back open wide
it gets inside
your body knows
the beat the beams
the siren flare across
a face a breath you taste
it if you if you want
it nothing here
can hurt you nothing
hiding in the air
the bodies nothing
to regret just listen
to the beat the heart
she says
forget forget forget

Rock Show in the Basement of St. Ignatius

When I see you see me
out of everyone
tonight
I'm burning clean
for a second.
I want to eat you,
hunched and suffering.
I want your eyes closed,
long hair hanging
in front of your face,
your sweat, your ribs
in your sallow skin.
I want to swallow you.
I want to follow you
out to the desert
wearing a crown
of lilies
in my hair.
I want these people
to see me shining
in a ring
of refracted glory.
See my face
in the crowd
and choose me.
Make me into the girl
who knows you.
Take me with you
wherever you're going
after this.

A Little Phrase, Designed to Go Unnoticed

We're at the Princeton Club,
me and a short man
who'd been bullied,
he said, a little,
after our conversation
had turned to the occult—
the hotline mediums of the mid-'90s
and their messages of hope,
late night, for the lonely kids
with credit card information,
on their third hour,
waiting to hear someone say
Come out, soft boy,
there is nothing to be afraid of.
There is love for you, fat girl,
written in the stars.

Last Drink With Dr. Manning

Shimmering godhead,
host of heavenly evenings,
play for us.
Some of the old ones from Sligo—
"Róisín Dubh" and "Isle of Innisfree."
Professor of reels and phenomena,
how we crane
at you, radiant, mixing drinks
for us, fervently seated
among your books
and African souvenirs.

The night before grades are due
you invite us here,
to this sanctum of loose tea
and aging timber. We can smell
your skin and talcum in the air.

The moment your mother died
a crucifix bloomed in bruise
across her chest, you tell us,
dramming out whiskey.
Drink this and think of her.

And we do.
Of her and of you,
your worn-out elbows and wild hair,
classroom gods and monsters,
all things seen and unseen,
all that whiskey can gather in girls
with their arms raised,
looking at you for the last time,
singing hosanna.

Xanthelasmata

It turns out his heart had always been a bomb.
His fortune was written in fatty glyphs
across the hollows of his eyes.
We should have seen that he was dying.

Our father's disfigurement bloomed
across his face like a sign to his sons,
a warning that what would kill them
was probably already forming inside them.

We should have seen that he was dying
but we were deep in a darkened cinema,
breathing the buttered air, watching Wednesday
and her extended family of ghouls.

In our home movies he's mostly behind the camera.
We started to look for his absence—
to look for us looking at him, or his hand
around the camcorder, shaking the shot,

or the blurry margins of a man being filmed by his children,
ringed by the halos of early '90s home recording,
his body subject to the shortcomings of VHS.
It's hard to tell, from what we have, what's dust

on the tape and what's the prophecy, the code
in the constellations across the orbits of his eyes
that meant he was born to leave his children.
His body was built to kill him young.

Flatland Tours

We ride the rangy center of the state
in a swamp buggy, twelve feet off the ground
on tractor tires and a salvaged chassis
with bucket seats bolted on.
I feel unsafe but scrappy. Strong.
The stubby copses shake—
there's something in the grass.
Wild hogs, perhaps.

We sway with the landscape, jolting
and roaring our way
through the fragile morning cold.
The old man steers with one hand
and shouts about smudge pots
he used to fire in the winter
to keep the freeze off his orange grove.

I admire the fierceness.
The sweetness of loving this land,
of trying to tame it. The squint-shrunk eyes
from a life in a ruthless climate.
The movement of reaching over a cow gate
so innate to the muscles of certain arms.

On the ranchland near Ocala
I think of the girls like the one I was.
So frizzy and round. Not quite
what their mothers imagined
and not quite at ease outdoors.

The old man floors the buggy.
The big thing lurches and lands
with a cocksure spray of loamy gray.
His hands are cracked and mapped
with years of his own mud.
He knows this land like he knows the beat
of his own blood.

Florida Field Guide

A dog-eared picture of sea grape hedges
we found in the crawlspace.
A cottonmouth snake.
A raccoon drinking
from a swimming pool.
A pig in the ground
and a family waiting to eat.
We scoop from her belly
and pile what we find on soft
yellow bread.

Off the port of Miami
our mother lists with the ship
as she leaves the bay for St. Lucia,
looking down from the deck at an ibis
plucking at roof tar. She remembers
she forgot her pills.

We crowd around the sow
as she blisters.

Cocoplum

The landfill passes for real land most of the time
but fat Floridian storms bring up the truth

about sea level and families
growing faster than the city.

The neighborhood used to be a beach.
The streets run with clipped grass and trash

and potting soil when it rains—
a network of temporary rivers.

The trees were planted to hold the ground.
The coastal forms are highly tolerant of salt.

The house is big and cold, with stiff rooms
for a quiet mother and two sisters living

in too much house, the space that's left
from a bigger family. The father is dead.

The rain pulls ferns in through the cracks
in the white stucco. The kitchen blooms

while exhausted pool floats fill with water
and then with tadpoles. The hammock grows

green mold in the crosses of its ropes
and leaves wet diamonds on their backs.

The dog is tied to the stove.
The heat steams the jalousie slats.

The doors swell up tight in their frames
but the girls never try to leave anyway.

Hale-Bopp

We might say the house drove us out.
Our hollow house, near-empty and echoing
with the murmur of infant insects,
forced us first out onto the lawn,
then out of the state.

The truth was something about the sound
and something about the solitude.
The wing dust in the corners.

The eastern lubbers laid thousands
of frothy, oblong eggs in tidy rows
beneath our feet. Great clouds
of grasshopper nymphs burst up in the heat,
accumulating in numbers and growing bigger,
growing yellow. Growing wings.

This was, of course, the comet spring.
A bright swipe of ice and star debris
tracked a slow path across the sky at night
and we were all turned up
like young stalks looking for light,
for ways to outgrow our mother,
watching the comet grow two bright tails
in Sagittarius.

We lived in the house
where our father had died,
where we learned what was possible
to sleep through.
When the humming got too loud
we'd go out and watch the comet.

We stayed up late on on the computers
in our bedrooms, bodies backlit,
learning new ways to be less lonely.
Learning new ways to leave the house.

The stars, it turned out, were already dead.
Our maps were just memories of light.
We were born hollow as houses and marked
with the ash of decimated planets.
We took the comet by the tail.
We decided our mother would be fine.

FIVE

Looking Down

This year the town blooms brackish
and buildings crack with salt. I think
I'd sink in an estuary I could swallow,
now I know that home
is where the lizards frill
for their diamond ladies
and that trees can shed their snakes
when they get full. But won't an ordinary hull
get thin and rusty? Won't the sunlight bend
our backs and slit our eyes? We all live, I guess,
with our decisions. I came to the city
like a clamshell tired of closing.
I looked for you like a mangrove
claws below the tide.

I Want Some Land

I want some loneliness justified by my location.
I want to purchase a piece of the earth.
To be in on that giant joke.
I want to put a fence around my family.
I want the burden of aging infrastructure.
The urge to complain about all the things
I own. I want the place to look overgrown.
Potted plants in the bathroom.
Big buxom banana leaves. Ferns.
I want an alarm. I want to love a place
 so much I install a siren.
I want a gut renovation.
Maintain some original details
without all the darkness and wasted space.
I want some land. I want the earth
and the sky above it.
I want the mineral rights, the air rights.
I want the right to take legal action
if someone encroaches on my boundaries.
I want to be right when I say
this whole damn thing is mine.

South of Marler

after Mary Oliver, for Paul Farmer

Late for pickup and zooming
through the Grove in my van
I try to be astonished
at the ferocious beauty
alongside the road.
The monstera, huge
and holy.
The screaming vines.
The palms
like beautiful women.
The daytime fox
that the neighbor feeds.
The lizard bobbing his head,
inflating his strawberry neck.
Looking for a friend.

I know
part of the work
of plants
is to confer dignity
on a place.
I drive under live oaks
older than America,
weaving their witch-
finger branches together
for me, forming
a spangled tunnel
over the minivan.
I know
I am lucky
to live in a place
deemed worthy
of so much dignity.
I am lucky
to know that lucky
isn't the right word.

After Rebmann and the Safari Collection Brochure

Like a bird in a restaurant
I've been transformed
by the walls around me
into a filthy thing,
a hovering problem
who moves too fast
and doesn't know how to leave.

Like the 10-foot alligator caught
in a Clearwater kitchen,
hissing and thrashing around
in a puddle of red wine and glass,
I've been monstrously wrong.
My fury's gone viral.
My body's been made absurd
for its size and for its suffering,
made available to subscribers.

Like the herd of giraffes
with their heads
through a hotel window
I want my beauty back.
I want to understand my rights
on either side of a given partition.
If a window implies permission,
turns me into a freaky background
for a stranger's vacation photos
I want to know.

Shake It

You can shake it
if you hate it.
You can shake it
if you learn to love yourself
or if you don't.

And you probably won't
but I think America
is ready for complexity.

Get next to me
at USPS
with your tax returns
and your Amazon returns.
We can still be mystics.

I saw God
and she told me
that you should still do
the big eyeliner.
She's said she's for you,
one hundred percent.

So you were a joke.
Your ex said
the sight of your naked body
made him soft.
We can still get mythical.

Shake it mama.
Get down
in your muscles,
with your memories,
with someone.

You know
you don't have to love it
to give it.
You don't have to feel like
you deserve it.

My Body Writes Me a Sonnet

Having coalesced around you, how I love you.
You are the one I breathe through the night for.
I take flesh in my mouth each day and chew
it into something that serves you, something more
than I can give you. I try to teach you what I know,
adopted child, about the past. The bone-bent grief
of the people who made you to survive in snow
you've never seen, to bare your teeth
at anyone getting too close to your kids
or your sweet, soft life. And all the times I endured
your laxatives and relaxers, I knew that you did
it to protect me, to make less of me to hate. Be sure
that I love you. And, of course, that I'll outlive you.
And you haven't asked, but of course, I forgive you.

Shelter As a Family

I was expecting more,
barometrically.
I thought I'd feel the weather
in my bones by now.
But here we are,
making cocktails,
making fun of ourselves
for getting so scared
of what has amounted
to intermittent rain.

We've been riding
the ragged edge of a crisis
all day.
Through nap time,
through screen time,
the storm's been slamming
the Abacos,
wailing on a woman
whose choices mirror mine—
who's wrapped her family
in Sheetrock and shingles
and prayed.

Today she's the one
who woke up
to the whistle.
She's the one
on the top bunk,
watching the ocean come up
through the floor.
I'm the one
making jokes
about building my life

in the Gulf Stream,
sending kisses
to people up north
from the cone of uncertainty.
Love from the outer bands.

Big Sugar

Head west in the burning season
through the cane fields
cleaned of vegetation,
lean, just stalks of sugar,
ready to ship.

Take 75 through the sawgrass,
relentlessly flat except
for cypress knees,
the guitar-shaped hotel,
the cinderblock clinic
outside of Immokalee,
the sugar mill flying
its smoke flags over Clewiston.

The coast will have to take you
as you are: your ashy car,
the black you blow from your nose,
what you drove through
to get here. It's part of you

by the time you get to Captiva.
The sound in a shell
is the sound of sugar in your blood
but you already knew that. Breathe
like the girls leaving the clinic.
Not clean, but new.

Retired Hurricane Names

Katrina hardly sounds
like a name anymore.
Two plosive pops and a bang
on the roof of the mouth.
It sounds like a storm.
Like Sandy, my father's name
before it was trash and silt
in the subway for miles, for years.
He's still an entity. Legally, technically.
There is land in the state of Florida
under the name of Sandy Block.
We were under a mattress
in Andrew—my mother,
sister, brother.
Dad was outside with the dead
and the meteorologists—
near-horizontal,
screaming at us
in their slickers:
Get Down, Get Close
to the Ground.
Andrew's a cartoon vortex,
flexing and blooming
two cumulus biceps,
glaring at Metro-Dade.
Maybe I saw that that in the paper.
Bryan Norcross said,
It's time to hunker down.
A hole in the storm
can turn your head around
and this is a glitchy landscape.
In Donna my grandfather drove around
to see what an American car
could handle.
Most deaths occur in the aftermath,

anyway—falling tree limbs,
rusty nails. Loose exotic pets.
It's easy to make a mistake.
A plastic sleeve is a snakeskin.
A snake is a hose.
A hose is a power line.
A piece of the flag on the ground
is a piece of an awning.
It's not a metaphor.

Notes

"Allegory with Human Host" references two nursery rhymes: "Hey Diddle Diddle" and "Froggy Went A' Courtin.'" It was written during the Zika virus outbreak in Miami in 2016.

The title of "The Mind Is Its Own Place" refers to Milton's *Paradise Lost*, Book 1, Lines 254-255: "The mind is its own place, and in it self / Can make a Heav'n of Hell, a Hell of Heav'n." The poem also makes reference to the November 1981 *Time* article of the same name.

"Crown Club Nights" responds to the exhibit "Party-ish" from the Womanish exhibit in Wynwood, Miami (ongoing). It was written as part of SWWIM's 2021 call for ekphrastic response.

"South of Marler" is dedicated to the late physician, anthropologist, and humanitarian Dr. Paul Farmer, a co-founder of the medical nonprofit Partners In Health (PIH) and the author's godfather. He was an avid proponent of the dignity-conferring qualities of plants and gardens and made sure that PIH's sites around the world were beautifully landscaped. Marler Avenue is the historic dividing line between the Bahamian settlement in Miami's Coconut Grove and the more affluent, historically white section of the neighborhood.

"After Rebmann and the Safari Collection Brochure" was written in response to the work of Miami-based surrealist Alena Rebmann.

The title of "Retired Hurricane Names" refers to the NOAA's practice of removing the names of especially deadly or destructive storms from their annual roster.

About the Author

Mary Block's poems have appeared in *Aquifer, Belleview Literary Review, Best New Poets 2020, The Florida Review Online, Mudfish, Nimrod International Journal, RHINO, Sonora Review, SWWIM Every Day*, and elsewhere. She is a graduate of New York University's Creative Writing Program, a Best of the Net finalist, a finalist for the Ruth Lilly Poetry Fellowship (now the Ruth Lilly and Dorothy Sargent Rosenberg Poetry Fellowship) from the Poetry Foundation, and a Pushcart Prize nominee. Mary lives in her hometown of Miami, Florida, with her spouse, two young children, and one old dachshund. She is an editor at SWWIM.

maryblock.net

About the Artist

Ali Mac is a Connecticut-based artist working across mediums. Her style is characterized by loose, organic lines and candy-colored hues. She discovered her love for sewing during the COVID-19 pandemic after inheriting her mom's old Singer. What began as a hobby making clothing appliqués for her first baby quickly evolved into animations and large scale portraits in sewn, layered felt. In addition to her felt work, Ali is a freelance illustrator and commercial artist with a client list including Harper Collins, Houghton Mifflin Harcourt, Penguin, and St. Martin's Press. She earned her MS in Communications Design from Pratt Institute.

alimacdoodle.com

Special Thanks

I owe enormous gratitude to my teachers, especially Mark Clark, Peter O'Connor, and the late Dom Damian Kearney, OSB at Portsmouth Abbey School; John Anderson, Amy Boesky, Paul Mariani, Robert Kern, and Kevin Ohi at Boston College; Sharon Olds, Major Jackson, Yusef Komunyakaa, Deborah Landau, and Rachel Zucker at New York University; and Sue Nichols, my kindergarten teacher.

To the SWWIM team: Catherine Esposito Prescott, Jen Karetnick, Caridad Moro-Gronlier, Alexandra Lytton Regalado, and Mia Leonin—I wish every poet had a crew like you. Thank you for sustaining me and giving me a place to belong when I moved home to Miami.

To the Miami Poetas Collective: Cat, Jen, Cary, Alex, Mia, Emma Trelles, Elisa Albo, and Rita Maria Martinez—thank you for showing up, even when the world shut down. I am so grateful for your insight and fellowship.

To Elaina Ellis, a trusted reader—thank you for your care with this manuscript and your faith in this project. You are an exceptionally gifted editor, and I'm grateful to have had the chance to work with you.

To the small-but-mighty team at The Word Works, especially Brad Richard and Nancy White—thank you for finding this book and believing in it. I'm thrilled to be a Word Works poet, and to have gotten to know you all throughout the process of bringing *Love from the Outer Bands* into the world.

To my best friend and creative partner, Ali Macdonald—thank you for making the felt hurricane happen. You are brilliant and I'm so lucky to know you.

To Fr. Scott O'Brien, OP; Fr. Jorge Presmanes, OP; and Fr. Mark Wedig, OP—thank you for the gift of your wisdom and love, and for giving my family and me a home within our faith. I am blessed to have been raised by Dominicans.

To my incredible family: my aunt, Laurie Weiss Nuell; Genevieve and Zisko Apaza; Chris and Catherine Block; Lizzi Nuell and Ryan Rosalsky; Robert and Tommy Nuell-Rivera; Molly Nuell and Tom Gallerani; Lynn Booth and Paul Monnin; and of course, the kids—Sander, Annabelle, Charley, Sophie, and AJ. Thank you for filling my life with enormous joy and fun, and for coming to my poetry readings.

To Peggy and Kent Herman, Caitlyn Herman and Austin Park, and Claire and Emilia—thank you for making me one of you. I love you.

To the great, extended Family Weiss: Lisa and Caron Cole; Sara Crawford, Jaidyn Garcia, and Tyler Garcia; Jillian Cole; Debbie Campbell & Rick Shimek; Marisa Campbell, Michael Estock and Nina Estock; Blake Campbell & Anai Fonte and Sawyer; Lane & Marta Abraham; Lissy Abraham; Loren & Lidia Abraham and Luke and Lyla Abraham; Cathy and Bob Berkowitz; Matt & Carla Berkowitz and Emile; Annie & Jordan Trachtenberg and Levi; Barry Bullock, Brandon & Ariel Bullock and Markeuise, Imani, and Raine; Myles Bullock; Richard Booth & Elena Padilla; Spencer Booth; Jeff Farmer; and Randi Silberman. I know Papa is so proud of us.

To Edward Block and Justine Block—thank you for your love and your stories about Sandy.

To my dead, especially my father, Jon Sander Block; Jay & Mary Beth Weiss; Paul Farmer; June Bullock; Joshua Bullock; and Austen Prescott—thank you for walking with me.

To my children, Jay and Daisy—I am so proud of you. Thank you for being proud of me, too.

And to Sean, my great love—thank you for the life we've built together. I'm so lucky to be spinning around in your orbit.

About The Word Works

Since its founding in 1974, The Word Works has steadily published volumes of contemporary poetry and presented public programs. Its imprints include The Washington Prize, The Tenth Gate Prize, The Hilary Tham Capital Collection, and International Editions.

Monthly, The Word Works offers free programs in its Café Muse Literary Salon. Starting in 2023, the winners of the Jacklyn Potter Young Poets Competition will be presented in the June Café Muse program.

As a 501(c)3 organization, The Word Works has received awards from the National Endowment for the Arts, the National Endowment for the Humanities, the D.C. Commission on the Arts & Humanities, the Witter Bynner Foundation, Poets & Writers, The Writer's Center, Bell Atlantic, the David G. Taft Foundation, and others, including many generous private patrons.

An archive of artistic and administrative materials in the Washington Writing Archive is housed in the George Washington University Gelman Library. The Word Works is a member of the Community of Literary Magazines and Presses.

wordworksbooks.org

Other Word Works Books

Annik Adey-Babinski, *Okay Cool No Smoking Love Pony*
Karren L. Alenier, *From the Belly: Poets Respond to Gerturude Stein's Tender Buttons* (ed.) / *Wandering on the Outside*
Nathalie Anderson, *Rough*
Emily August, *The Punishments Must Be a School*
Jennifer Barber, *The Sliding Boat Our Bodies Made*
Andrea Carter Brown, *September 12*
Willa Carroll, *Nerve Chorus*
Grace Cavalieri, *Creature Comforts* / *The Long Game: Poems Selected & New*
Abby Chew, *A Bear Approaches from the Sky*
Nadia Colburn, *The High Shelf*
Henry Crawford, *The Binary Planet*
Barbara Goldberg, *Berta Broadfoot and Pepin the Short* / *Breaking & Entering: New and Selected Poems*
Akua Lezli Hope, *Them Gone*
Michael Klein, *The Early Minutes of Without: Poems Selected & New*
Deborah Kuan, *Women on the Moon*
Frannie Lindsay, *If Mercy*
Elaine Magarrell, *The Madness of Chefs*
Chloe Martinez, *Ten Thousand Selves*
Marilyn McCabe, *Glass Factory*
JoAnne McFarland, *Identifying the Body*
Leslie McGrath, *Feminists Are Passing from Our Lives*
Kevin McLellan, *Ornitheology*
Ron Mohring, *The Boy Who Reads in the Trees*
A. Molotkov, *Future Symptoms*
Ann Pelletier, *Letter That Never*
W. T. Pfefferle, *My Coolest Shirt*
Ayaz Pirani, *Happy You Are Here*
Robert Sargent, *Aspects of a Southern Story* / *A Woman from Memphis*
Roger Smith, *Radiation Machine Gun Funk*
Jeddie Sophronius, *Love & Sambal*
Julia Story, *Spinster for Hire*
Leah Umansky, *Of Tyrant*
Barbara Ungar, After *Naming the Animals*
Cheryl Clark Vermeulen, *They Can Take It Out*
Julie Marie Wade, *Skirted*
Miles Waggener, *Superstition Freeway*
Fritz Ward, *Tsunami Diorama*
Camille-Yvette Welsch, *The Four Ugliest Children in Christendom*
Amber West, *Hen & God*
Maceo Whitaker, *Narco Farm*

www.ingramcontent.com/pod-product-compliance
Lightning Source LLC
Chambersburg PA
CBHW032010080426
42735CB00007B/561